RETAIL MASTERY

UNLOCK THE SECRET TO
3X FOOTFALLS & HIGHER PROFITS

RETAIL MASTERY

UNLOCK THE SECRET TO 3X FOOTFALLS & HIGHER PROFITS

Amit Singhal

Worldwide Published by
Pendown Press

PENDOWN PRESS LLP

An ISO 9001 & ISO 14001 Certified Co.,

Regd. Office: 3767A, Kanhaiya Nagar,

Tri Nagar, Delhi-110035

Ph.: 8130886000, 9650072927

E-mail: info@pendownpress.com

Branch Office: 1A/2A, 20, Hari Sadan, Ansari Road,

Daryaganj, New Delhi-110002

Ph.: 011-45794768

Website: PendownPress.com

Edition: 2024

Price: ₹ 399

ISBN: 978-93-6338-932-8

Layout and Cover Designed by Pendown Graphics Team

Printed and Bound in India by Thomson Press India Ltd.

CONTENTS

FOREWORD

Amit is among my earliest professional associates, we have been bouncing boards to each other for nearly 30 years. I have been a witness to his development from an astute B-to-B professional to an enabler of B-to-C sales, mirroring the development of Branded Fashion Retail in India.

Amit has embarked on a courageous journey as an author trying to throw light on the fundamentals of retail which are hidden in plain sight.

By very nature, Amit is meticulously detail oriented which has come in handy in creating this book on retail embodying the adage–

"Retail is Detail".

The book will do real service to practitioners of retail who are so engrossed in the everyday challenges of nuts and bolts that the critical differentiators miss their attention. This book will bridge that gap.

Nikhil Mohan
Founder & Director
Blackberrys

ACKNOWLEDGEMENTS

My first book is the result of a long-held manifestation.

It has been possible due to the inspiration and motivation of my well-wishers who have helped me in this journey.

Life is an educational institution and we are lifelong learners. We inspire others to aspire and vice-versa. This inspirational journey would be incomplete sans my gratitude towards those who made it possible by their presence in my life.

The journey of over three decades would not have been possible without the strong support and blessings of my loving father, Late Sh. Dharam Prakash Singhal, who was my first coach in the world of retailing and who taught me the ethics and nitty-gritty of the business.

I would like to express my heartfelt gratitude -

- To you, the reader, for giving it your precious time and attention. It is for you that I do what I do. A heartfelt thank you for your endless love and support.
- To my first mentor, Mr. Nikhil Mohan at Blackberrys, who in our almost 30 years of association has provided me with valuable insights and shared his infinite wisdom with me over the years. He has for many years been my idol and the person I look up to. Thank you sir dil se.
- To my friend, mentor, coach and the ultimate marketing guru Akshar Yadav, who propelled and guided me into writing this book. Without his persistence and push, I wouldn't have moved an inch towards writing this book. Akshar bhai dil se dhanyavaad.
- To my sister, Aparna Jain, for being the first person to proofread this book and provide me with excellent inputs on the manuscript.

- To my friend and publisher, Dinesh Verma, for taking the load off my shoulders. Dinesh bhai is responsible for the cover design, final edit and proofreading, follow up and publishing of this book.
- To my friends, Anurag, Sandeep, Deepak, Rajiv, Kamal, Chandan, Sanjay and Sachin, for listening to all the chatter and endless questions related to the content.
- Most of all, to the most special person in my life – my friend, my girlfriend and YES, my wife Shalini. Her belief in me and her child-like enthusiasm helped me steer the pathways of doubt that came along the journey.
- To my two children Utkarsh & Medhya, who helped me along and for their love, support and understanding of the long hours, the sacrificed weekends and the canceled vacations.

You are all the light that shows me the way.

❑❑❑

"It's time to start living the life you've imagined"

- Henry James -

"Every second is a chance
To turn your life around"

- Unknown -

"A Comfort zone is a beautiful place
But nothing ever grows there"

- John Assaraf -

If we did all the things that we are capable of doing,
we would literally astound ourselves.

- Thomas A Edison -

"Progress is impossible without change and those who
cannot change their minds cannot change anything"

- George Bernard Shaw -

PROLOGUE

MY JOURNEY
In Search of the Future

Have you ever wandered into a store and felt its buzzing energy hit you like a force of nature?

Every corner of the store feels alive and inviting as if it wants to embrace you and include you in its story. Your sense of hearing is engaged with the sound of laughter, deep conversation between the staff & customers and the rustle of shopping bags.

Next, you are in for a visual treat as you take in the shelves & displays brimming with carefully curated products, arranged attractively and invitingly.

This is not just any store, a place where you merely come to shop; this is an experience, a journey of discovery, finding treasures that bring a sparkle to your eyes and a spring to your step.

Such a store is not just a place where you go to buy things, it's a place for relaxing, a productive and soulful experience.

Contrast this with another scene: a store that is not very well lit or is too harshly lit, the environment is silent except for the lonely echo of a shop assistant's footsteps.

The products, though plentiful, aren't arranged invitingly and the overall vibe of the store doesn't feel warm and welcoming.

Which store would you buy from consistently?

Obviously, this is a no-brainer!

This, dear retail business owners, is a stark but real illustration of the retail divide - separated not by luck but by one business owner's understanding of what truly drives success in retail and the other's lack of it.

The difference is not magic!

It's not some mystical retail spell; it's all about mastering the fundamentals of retail, those hidden gems that can turn a store from "forgettable" to "unforgettable".

My First Love

The vibrant silks and intricate embroidery of my father's saree showroom weren't just a backdrop to my childhood; they were the first seeds of my lifelong love affair with retail.

Witnessing the joy on a customer's face after finding the perfect saree, for whom it was a manifestation of their dreams and a medium of expression, ignited a spark within me

– the spark of understanding the power of retail to transform not just appearances, but lives.

I recall a particular customer, a young woman who walked into the store with a timid aura and was transformed before my eyes. She entered the store with uncertainty, her eyes scanning the myriad of options with a sense of overwhelm.

However, with gentle guidance, she was introduced to a sari that seemed to be made just for her. The moment she draped it around her, her entire demeanor changed. She stood taller, her eyes sparkled with confidence, and her smile radiated pure joy.

It was a transformative experience, not just for her but for me as well.

It was then that I understood the true power of retail –

it wasn't merely about transactions; it was about creating moments of joy and empowerment.

Having grown up with the store as my playground, finally taking the first plunge felt natural, like a fish diving into crystal-clear water

However, as I assisted with sales and observed customer interactions, I began sensing a limitation. The intimacy of a single store, while valuable, couldn't reach the vast audience I yearned to connect with.

The desire to share the magic of retail on a larger scale bloomed within me.

My heart longed to bring about a transformation in the lives of many and help other retailers rediscover the magic of retail.

So, with a heart full of ambition and a head armed with the wisdom of lessons learned, I embarked on a new adventure - building my own retail business.

But as I ventured beyond the comforting walls of the family showroom, I saw a completely different picture.

Most stores everywhere seemed to be focused only on trying to lure in customers. Their motive was merely transactional, they did not endeavor to serve and go the extra mile.

It was like watching a chef attempt to bake a cake without flour – the result was bound to be a half-baked disaster.

These stores were focusing so much on short-term gains that they were neglecting the fundamentals of retail – the very elements that could make them stand out and thrive.

However, what truly struck me and stayed with me over the course of my 30+ years in this dynamic industry is a recurring problem. Most retailers, caught in the whirlwind of daily operations, are laser-focused solely on increasing sales figures.

Sales- this singular metric is undoubtedly important, however, allowing it to overshadow the fundamental wheels that underpin true retail success is a blunder.

It pained me to witness talented retailers struggling because they lacked a strong foundation. Their focus on short-term gains neglected the long-term sustainability of their businesses. Witnessing their struggles fueled a burning desire within me – to help, to empower.

The journey wasn't without its challenges. There were long nights spent strategizing, and then came the hurdles in navigating the intricacies of supply chains, and the constant learning curve of keeping pace with ever-evolving consumer trends.

I did not let the obstacles stop me and I embarked on a journey of learning, learning from the masters themselves on retailing, happiness, business and training to be better equipped to solve the pain of my retailers. To help them bring a transformation in their lives.

And that's where this book, and my extended commitment, come in.

Through years of careful observation, I've delved into the very heart of retail - the often-overlooked little things that make a difference, from understanding staff behavior and motivation to analyzing owner perspectives and so many subtle details.

So, after 30 years spent hands-on in the field of retail, from witnessing the rise and fall of brands to navigating through the ever-changing trends, and every mistake a store can make, I've decided to share the secrets I've uncovered. I've also seen the **power of the right approach.**

This book is your secret weapon!

Imagine a store where customers don't just come and go, but linger, explore, and leave with a smile, where each product tells a compelling story, and where the ambience is so inviting that people can't help but return. Picture a team that's not just clocking in hours, but is genuinely excited to be a part of your success. This isn't a pipe dream; it's a tangible reality that's within your reach. And it all starts with this book.

This book is your gateway to transforming your store.

It is your compass, a guide to mastering the core principles of retail. It delves into the essential strategies that I've witnessed work wonders, transforming struggling businesses into thriving hubs of customer satisfaction and financial success.

It equips you to identify areas of improvement within your retail journey and unlock the potential for exponential business growth. It is more than just a guide; it's a companion on your journey to retail excellence, to help you unlock the true potential of your store.

Ready to unlock your store's true potential?

This book is just the beginning; My support extends beyond the pages of this book. I believe in fostering a community of empowered retailers, a network of individuals who can learn from each other and collaborate towards shared success.

As you turn these pages, you'll find not just strategies and tips, but stories, experiences, and real-life examples that will guide you every step of the way. Let's dive in, and together, we'll unlock the true potential of your store. And remember, I'm here to support you every step of the way.

Connect with me via email (amit@facetsgroup.net) and let's embark on this journey together. I'm committed to standing by your side, offering guidance and celebrating your victories.

Welcome to your retail evolution!

Partnering your retail success

Sincerely,

Amit

CHAPTER 1

GETTING STARTED

The Driving Wheels of Retail Success

Imagine yourself standing at a bustling intersection.

Customers are the cars, zipping past shop windows, drawn in by some and ignoring others.

Amidst all this competition, your store needs to not only catch their attention but compel them to stop, explore, and ultimately, buy.

This is the essence of successful retail. It's not just about selling products, it's about creating an experience that compels customers to choose you over your competitors.

But how does one do that and what are the building blocks for creating this experience?

As promised above it's now time for me to share with you the learnings that will transform your retail business from surviving to thriving, so let's get started without any further ado....

In this chapter, I detail the four foundational wheels that will drive your business to success, smoothly and speedily

The Four Wheels of Retail Excellence

I want you to envision your retail business as a grand chariot or your favourite luxury/sports car (whatever your preference). To move forward smoothly and efficiently, all four wheels need to be perfectly aligned, right?

Similarly, there are four crucial wheels that are the foundation of retail which support and drive retail success.

If you want your business vehicle to have a smooth forward journey, you will need to focus on each one of these and keep them in alignment.

1. Visual Merchandising

This wheel is all about creating a visually appealing store environment that attracts customers, showcases your products in the best light, and influences buying decisions. It revolves around sculpting a store environment that is not only visually eye-catching but also strategically arranged to spotlight your products, making them irresistible to prospective buyers.

The art and science of visual merchandising lies in utilizing space, color, lighting, and layout to tell a compelling story about your products, one that secretly whispers and yet shouts out, to the desires and aspirations of your customers.

2. Staff Training and Empowerment

The second wheel represents the chariot's heart or the car's engine—the team driving it. Happy, knowledgeable, and empowered staff are the lifeblood of any retail business. They are the ones who interact directly with customers (and are the first face of your business), build relationships, and ultimately close the sale. Their ability to understand, engage, inform, and inspire customers can transform a regular purchase into a memorable experience, building loyalty and trust that extend far beyond a single transaction.

3. Data Analytics

The third wheel forms the chariot's navigational compass/your car's GPS, guiding its journey through the vast landscape of consumer behavior. In today's data-driven world, understanding your customers and their buying behavior is key. By analyzing sales data, customer demographics, and other relevant information, retailers can make informed decisions about their inventory, marketing strategies, and overall operations, ensuring that your store remains a relevant and enticing destination for your target audience.

4. **Effective Communication**

   The fourth and final wheel represents the chariot's connection to the outside world. Clear and consistent communication, both internally with your staff and externally with your customers and vendors, is essential for building trust and fostering loyalty. Effective communication builds a bridge of trust and transparency, essential for nurturing a loyal customer base and a cohesive, motivated team. Remember, a clear call to action, like a friendly shop assistant offering assistance, ensures customers know exactly how you can help them.

These four wheels are interconnected and work together to create a strong foundation for retail success. By mastering the working of each wheel and ensuring they are aligned with each other, you can create a retail experience that stands out from the crowd and drives your business forward.

In the following chapters, we'll delve deeper into each of these four wheels, sharing practical strategies and real-world examples to help you implement them effectively in your retail business.

By drawing upon your experience, incorporating the insights presented here, and continuously seeking to improve, you can build a retail experience that makes customers "click" – connecting them with your brand and driving them back for more.

The possibilities are endless – let's embark on this journey together and unlock the true potential of your store.

❑❑❑

CHAPTER 2

CAPTIVATE YOUR CUSTOMERS

The Power of 5 Senses in Retail

THE GIFT OF THE SENSES

When GOD created humans, HE blessed them with 5 special gifts - The Five Senses: Sight, Sound, Smell, Touch & Taste.

Then HE told them "Go and explore the world with these gifts".

Ever since humans have been led by the 5 senses and continue to live their lives governed by them.

Have you ever walked past a store window and been instantly drawn in? Or entered a store and felt a certain ambience that made you linger and explore? These are the subtle yet powerful effects of **visual merchandising.**

WHAT IS VISUAL MERCHANDISING?

Visual merchandising is the art of creating a visually appealing and engaging retail experience.

It's about showcasing your products in a way that entices customers, tells a story about your brand, and ultimately, drives sales.

The memory of the **5 senses plays** an important role in the buying patterns of the customers. All experiences influenced by the **5 senses** are stored in the memory, thereby impacting their decision-making.

In this chapter, we'll delve into the **5 senses**, the hidden forces that influence our shopping behavior and how you, as a retailer, can use them to your advantage.

The 5 Senses in Action

Think of each sense as a piece of a puzzle, contributing to the overall customer experience.

Let's explore each one and how you can leverage it in your retail space:

1. **Sight:** 'Beauty lies in the eyes of the beholder' is an oft-used quote which exemplifies our shopping experience. "The Sense of Sight" is heightened at the offset of any shopping experience and determines if a customer will enter a store. This is the first impression and often the most crucial.

    - **Window displays:** Your window is your 3-second advertisement. Remember, you only have a few seconds to grab their attention, so make it memorable. Create eye-catching displays that showcase your products and brand story. Use vibrant colors, creative lighting, and storytelling elements. Remember your window is the first 3-second advertisement of your store.
    - **Store layout:** Design a layout that is easy to navigate and guides customers through your merchandise. Don't just display products; create a narrative. Use mannequins to showcase outfits, not just clothes.
    - **Aesthetics:** Pay attention to details like color schemes, lighting, and the overall presentation of your products and staff presentation.

    For example, you can use bright or warm colors to attract attention and create excitement, or use contrast to highlight important features or messages. You can also use shapes that match your brand personality or product category, such as curves for softness and femininity, or angles for strength and masculinity. All these play a major role in inviting the customer inside.

2. **Smell:** Subtle fragrances can create a positive atmosphere and influence emotions. A pleasant aroma, like freshly brewed coffee in a clothing store, can create a positive first impression and influence customer behavior.
    - **Choose scents that complement your brand and products.** For example, a nicely stocked fragrance/perfume counter at the entry of the store that gives a whiff of fresh fragrance.
    - **Avoid overpowering scents that can be unpleasant or overwhelming.** The scent of the store, staff, clothes and furnishing also profoundly impacts the customer. Especially the foul-smelling mouth of a staff member having indulged in pan masala/ cigarettes really puts a customer off. Also taking care of any foul smell emanating in the store due to whatever reason like smelly washrooms & dirty housekeeping etc.
3. **Sound:** The melodies of the store play an important role in the buying process. The background music, the humdrum of the store staff, and their etiquette of communication with each other and the customer are the areas that would need your attention. The right music can set the mood and influence customer behavior.
    - **Upbeat music can energize shoppers** and encourage them to browse, while **calming melodies can encourage them to linger** and explore further.
    - **Consider the demographics of your target audience** when selecting background music.

4. **Touch:**

"Often the hands will solve a mystery that the intellect has struggled with in vain"- Carl Jung.

Allowing customers to interact with your products creates a deeper connection. Upon touching a surface that is dusty or oily (as in a restaurant) the customer is left with a sense of disquiet and displeasure. On the contrary, the touch of clean crockery & cutlery as well as crisp table cloths can enhance the experience. The touch of the fabric, tables, furnishings, seating, and textures all lend to conditioning the mind to buy.

- **Arrange products in a way that invites customers to touch and feel them.** This is especially important for items like clothing and home goods.
- **Ensure your products and shelves are clean and well-maintained** to create a positive impression. A point to note here is the corners of the tables and displays, which should not be edgy or broken and may hurt the customer or their kids.
- **Encourage customers to interact with your products.**

5. **Taste:** While primarily used in the food and beverage industry, offering samples can create a positive association with your brand and encourage repeat visits.

- This doesn't have to be limited to F&B retail.
- Every retail store can engage the sense of taste of their customers by offering them candies, chocolates etc. either in-store or by surprising them with these gifts in their shopping bags.
- You can also offer them hot/cold beverages such as tea, coffee, iced tea, sparkling water, juices, lemonade etc. as per the season.

Beyond the Senses

While the 5 senses play a crucial role, remember that visual merchandising is about creating a **cohesive and engaging** experience for your customers.

Here are a few pro-pointers to take your VM to the next level and truly up your retail game.

- **Storytelling:** Use your displays and product placement to tell a story about your brand and the lifestyle you represent.
- **Consistency:** Ensure your visual merchandising is consistent throughout your store, from the window displays to the fitting rooms.
- **Regular updates:** Keep your displays fresh and updated to reflect seasonal changes and new product arrivals.
- **Focus on customer experience:** Think about how your visual merchandising makes your customers feel and how it guides them through their shopping journey.
- **Be creative and experiment:** Don't be afraid to try new things and step outside your comfort zone.
- **Track and analyze results:** Monitor what works and what doesn't, and adapt your strategies based on data and customer feedback.

By harnessing the power of the 5 senses and going beyond the basics, you can create a truly captivating retail experience that fosters positive customer interactions, and lasting connections with your customers and drives sales success.

Remember, each sense plays a unique role in shaping their perception, influencing purchasing decisions, and building brand loyalty.

Incorporate The Power of Storytelling In your Strategy

While captivating displays and strategic product placement are crucial, remember that **a successful retail experience goes beyond aesthetics.** To truly connect with your customers, your visual merchandising needs to tell a story – a story about your brand, your products, and the experience you offer.

Remember that a successful retail performance requires more than just an attractive display. It necessitates a well-trained and enthusiastic team to bring your vision to life.

In the next chapter, we'll delve deeper into the art of storytelling, exploring strategies to use staff training as a powerful tool to bring your visual narratives to life.

We'll also discuss how to empower your team to become brand ambassadors, effectively engaging with customers and weaving the story of your brand into every interaction.

❑❑❑

CHAPTER 3

THE UNTAPPED POTENTIAL

Empowering Your Staff for Retail Success

The Power of Storytelling

To be honest, when I use the word storytelling in a book on retail success, some of you may even be wondering; why.

Well, storytelling is one of the most powerful tools you can leverage to drive retail sales.

So, what is storytelling?

Have you ever asked this question with respect to your retail business?

WHAT IS STORYTELLING?

Storytelling is the art of creatively using narratives to build an emotional connection with your customers that creates an impact on their minds so that they may spend wholeheartedly, shopping to their heart's content.

Emotion is a powerful motivator of consumer behavior, as it influences how customers perceive, evaluate, and remember your brand and products.

It is an established fact that people don't merely buy products, they buy emotions.

To trigger emotion with storytelling, you need to create a narrative that connects your brand or products with your customers' needs, values, and aspirations. For example, you can use stories that appeal to universal themes such as love, family, adventure, or achievement, or use stories that relate to specific customer segments or contexts, such as millennials, mothers, or travelers.

Memory, as I mentioned earlier too, is a crucial factor in consumer behavior, as it determines how customers recall and recognize your brand and products when they are ready to make a purchase.

Memory is influenced by how customers encode and store information in their brains, which depends on how often and how meaningfully they are exposed to your marketing efforts.

As human beings, we tend to remember stories and visuals more than spoken content. So, it becomes imperative to create an impressive story that can leave a lasting impression on customer memory.

> "Marketing is no longer about the stuff that you sell, but about the stories you tell."
>
> **- Seth Godin**

To introduce storytelling in your retail business, **the first thing to do is to identify what is your story as a retailer**, as well as ask yourselves the following questions and answer them:

- What message do you want to convey?
- What is your legacy?
- What causes do you believe in and support?
- Is there something unique about your products?
- Do you have an ethical or sustainability mission?
- Are customers doing or achieving interesting things with your products?

- Do you have a **Selfie wall** for your customers to take pictures?
- What extra services or experiences do you offer to customers?
- Do you have a long/ interesting history behind your business?

Now that you know the guidelines for building a story around your brand/ products, you also need to understand the things that are a **strict NO-NO** in storytelling:

- Lying for the sake of profit
- Emotional manipulation
- Exaggerating what your store can do to trick consumers
- Bragging about how amazing your store is (without backing up those claims), basically committing what you cannot deliver.

Once you understand the power of storytelling and start building stories, the next logical question is how are these stories going to be delivered. Well, apart from the marketing material such as ads, brochures, websites, social media etc., the most important & impactful resource that will deliver these stories is your human resource; your staff.

Beyond Transactions: The Importance of Staff Training

Retailing isn't just about ringing up sales; it's about creating memorable customer experiences. But achieving this goal hinges on a crucial aspect often overlooked: **staff training.**

To truly thrive, retailers need to **empower their staff** to become **customer experience architects.** This shift in perspective from transactional selling to **experiential selling** is what sets successful retailers apart.

In the world of retail, your staff are the frontline heroes, directly influencing customer experience and ultimately, your bottom line.

Here's why staff training is the spark that ignites retail success:

- **Empowers Your Team:** Training equips your staff with the knowledge and skills they need to confidently navigate customer interactions, answer questions effectively, handle objections skillfully and handle various situations gracefully. This empowers them to take ownership of their roles and contribute more significantly to the team's success.
- **Enhances Customer Experience:** The core of staff training is their happiness quotient. A happy and contented team is the key to happy and satisfied customers. Well-trained staff can anticipate customer needs, provide personalized service, and build rapport. This translates to a more enjoyable and satisfying shopping experience for your customers, fostering loyalty and encouraging repeat visits.
- **Boosts Sales and Profitability:** Investing in employee development demonstrates your commitment to their growth and well-being. This fosters a positive work environment and reduces employee turnover, leading to a more stable and motivated workforce. Studies show that businesses with well-trained staff experience increased sales, and improved customer satisfaction, which translates to a significant boost in your bottom line.

Beyond the Basics: Key Training Areas

While product knowledge is an essential part of staff training, a comprehensive training program should encompass various key aspects such as:

- **Product Expertise:** Training equips your staff with the knowledge and skills they need to confidently navigate customer interactions, objections and any situations that may crop up smoothly. This empowers them to take ownership of their roles, answer customer questions confidently and guide them towards the right purchase.

- **Customer Service Excellence:** Foster a culture of exceptional customer service. This includes active listening, building rapport, effective communication, and conflict resolution strategies. necessary to deliver exceptional service to every customer.
- **Company Policies and Procedures:** Ensure your staff understand company policies, procedures, and expectations related to customer interactions, cash handling, and store operations.

Investing in your staff's training is not an expense, it's an investment in your business's future. By empowering and equipping them with the necessary skills, tools and knowledge they need to excel, you create a team to become valuable assets poised to ignite sales excellence and deliver exceptional customer experiences.

Remember, happy and empowered employees create **memorable customer experiences,** leading to a thriving and sustainable business.

The other important thing in training your staff is to make them understand the role they play in the customer's buying journey.

We as retailers have to ensure that our sole purpose in the shop is to be of service and not to sell. Sales is an automatic by-product of great service. The staff has to thoroughly understand the science of handling customer objections in such a manner that they help customers make informed decisions about their purchases.

However, knowledge without action is like a beautiful store window without engaging displays. To truly **transform** your retail space, you need to **connect with your customers on a deeper level**, understand their needs, and address them effectively.

In the next chapter, we'll delve into the world of data analysis. We'll explore how effectively **harnessing the power of data** can equip you with the insights needed to understand your customers, personalize their experience, refine your marketing strategies, optimize product offerings, analyze customer feedback and ultimately, **drive long-term business success.**

By **transforming data into actionable insights,** you can **refine your training programs, identify areas for improvement, and ensure your team continues to be the driving force behind your retail success story.**

❑❒❑

CHAPTER 4

THE LANGUAGE OF DATA
A Retailer's Love Story

In the world of retail, data is not just numbers on a spreadsheet; it's the lifeblood of your business. Like a **central nervous system**, data provides vital information about every aspect of your operations, from sales trends and customer behavior to staff performance and inventory management, allowing you to make informed decisions and achieve success

Harnessing the Power of Data Analysis

Traditionally retailers did not understand the importance of data and the treasures hidden within, all they cared about was the cash register and the stock-taking.

However, times have changed and retailers have begun to understand the importance of data & analytics derived from that data.

Today's retailers who embrace data analysis unlock a competitive advantage. By **deciphering the insights** hidden within the numbers, you can make informed decisions across various areas such as:

- **Staff Optimization:** Analyze **sales data** by salesperson or department to identify areas for improvement, develop targeted training programs and optimize staffing strategies.
- **Smarter Merchandising:** Data-driven sales insights enable you to identify trends, optimize pricing strategies, and target your marketing efforts effectively. Analyze **category-wise data** to understand customer preferences and optimize your **merchandise planning,**

ensuring you have the right merchandise in the right place at the right time. This translates to increased sales, improved margins, and ultimately, a healthier bottom line.

- **Cost Control:** Analyze data on **rental costs, salaries, electricity, and other operational expenses** to identify areas for cost-saving opportunities.
- **Customer-Centric Marketing:** Analyze **customer data** to understand buying behavior, preferences, pain points and demographics. This allows you to tailor your offerings, personalize your communication, and ultimately, build stronger customer relationships.
- **Profitability Analysis:** Analyze **sales data** alongside **purchase costs and head-wise operational expenses,** to gain a clear picture of your profit margins and identify areas for improvement. By making data-driven decisions in all areas of your business, you can optimize your operational costs and ultimately, increase profitability.

Beyond the Numbers: Asking the Right Questions

Numbers alone can't give you all the insights needed to drive business success. Data is gold and can give you direction.

Effective use of data starts with asking the right questions.

Clarity of thought is key.

- What areas of your business need the most attention?
- What specific information do you need to make informed decisions?
- What specific data points will provide the most valuable insights?

Remember, **it's not just about "what" happened, but also "why" and "how" it happened, and what might happen in the future.**

Often, businesses get caught up in simply analyzing "what happened" without delving deeper into **"why" and "how"** it happened.

This is where **data science** comes into play. While vast amounts of data are collected and readily available, true wisdom lies in extracting meaningful insights. By analyzing these aspects, you can use data to predict trends and proactively adapt your strategies.

By **embracing data-driven decision-making** and **utilizing the power of data analysis,** you can unlock valuable insights and gain a competitive edge in the ever-evolving retail landscape.

You can transform your retail business from a data-blind operation to a data-driven powerhouse, making informed decisions that drive growth and success.

From Data-Driven Insights to the Symphony of Communication

The power of data analysis empowers you to understand your customers, staff, and overall retail ecosystem on a deeper level, uncovering their preferences, motivations, and buying patterns. By deciphering the insights hidden within the numbers, you can make informed decisions, optimize operations, and refine your strategies for sustainable growth.

In the next chapter, we'll shift the focus from data to the melody of communication. We'll delve into the art of crafting **magnetic messages that speak directly to your target audience.** You'll learn how to leverage data-driven insights to create targeted marketing campaigns, personalize customer interactions, and craft in-store signage that speaks directly to your customers' wants and needs. **By harmonizing your data insights with the power of effective communication,** you'll be well-equipped to orchestrate a retail symphony that captivates your customers and drives sustainable growth.

❑❒❑

CHAPTER 5

COMMUNICATION IN RETAIL
Resonating with Customers and Staff

Imagine your retail store as a bustling marketplace, filled with customers and staff. Products gently whisper their features, displays silently tell stories, and music sets the mood.

However, without clear and effective communication, this symphony of sights and sounds can quickly become a cacophony, leaving your customers confused and frustrated.

The Importance of the "C" Word

In the world of retail, effective communication is **not a luxury, it's a necessity**. It's the bridge that connects you, the retailer, with your customers, your staff, and your suppliers, ensuring a smooth and satisfying experience. It encompasses all forms of interaction, from product descriptions and signage to staff interactions and customer service. When communication falters, the entire "symphony" of your business can suffer.

The Many Voices of Retail Communication

Effective communication in retail isn't just about one-way exchanges. it's a dynamic exchange between two persons. It's a multi-layered symphony with distinct "instruments":

- **Customer Communication:** This is the heart of the retail experience. From greeting customers warmly to answering inquiries patiently and resolving issues promptly, every interaction sets the tone for loyalty and repeat business. Clear communication builds trust and ensures customer satisfaction. By actively listening to their needs and concerns, you can address them effectively and foster positive relationships.

- **Staff Communication:** Clear communication with your team is vital. Ensure everyone understands their roles, company policies, and the overall vision. Regular meetings, open communication channels, and constructive feedback foster a positive and productive work environment.

  Train them in active listening, clear and concise communication, and the ability to explain product features and benefits effectively. Encourage them to build rapport with customers and answer questions confidently. When information flows freely, your staff feels valued and engaged. They can confidently answer customer questions, address concerns, and contribute their ideas, leading to a more positive and productive work environment.

- **Supplier Communication:** If your products are the soul of your store, then your suppliers are the backbone of your operations. It is vital for your backbone to be strong and upright for you as a business to stand tall. Building strong relationships with suppliers requires transparent and timely communication. Be clear about your expectations, manage lead times effectively, and maintain open dialogues to ensure smooth operations and product availability.

- **Visual Communication:** Product packaging, signage, window displays, and even the overall layout of your store all contribute to visual communication. Ensure they are clear, concise, and visually appealing, guiding customers effortlessly through your offerings.

- **Written Communication:** This includes everything from product descriptions on your website to printed receipts and marketing materials. Ensure your written communication is grammatically correct, easy to understand, and reflects your brand voice.

Beyond Words: Mastering the Art of Communication

Effective communication goes beyond just spoken words. Here are some key aspects to consider:

- **Active Listening:** Pay close attention to both verbal and nonverbal cues when interacting with your team, vendors and customers. This demonstrates genuine interest and helps you understand their needs and concerns effectively. Respond to inquiries and feedback promptly and professionally.
- **Clarity and Conciseness:** Communicate clearly and concisely using language everyone understands. Avoid jargon and technical terms that might create confusion.
- **Positive Body Language:** Maintain eye contact, smile appropriately, and use open body language to convey confidence and openness.
- **Empathy:** Put yourself in the shoes of your team members and customers. This fosters understanding and allows you to tailor your communication approach accordingly.

Communication Channels for Retail Success

1. **Regular Team Meetings:** Hold regular team meetings to discuss goals, challenges, and feedback. Encourage open communication and celebrate successes as a team.
2. **Performance Reviews:** Conduct regular performance reviews with your staff to provide feedback, address concerns, and offer opportunities for growth and development.
3. **Customer Feedback Surveys:** Gather feedback from customers through surveys to understand their experience and identify areas for improvement.

Some questions that you can ask your customer to gather data are ;

- What can we as a retailer do better to serve you and make your experience better?

- What type of Communication Suits you?
- What makes you come here often?
- What is it that you like about us?
- What makes you feel good about buying?
- What is it that you expect more from us?
- What can we do to make you buy more?

These questions when asked in a conversational format will get responses that will help you make informed decisions that are purely customer-centric

The 1 Thing that is a Strict NO as part of any Communication for you, your team or anybody associated with your store on the floor;

NEVER EVER ARGUE

Remember that you can never get the patronage of any customer by proving them wrong. Your goal is to help the customer make an informed decision.

By fostering a culture of open and effective communication, you can create a harmonious symphony in your retail space. Your staff will feel valued, your customers will be satisfied, and your business will thrive.

Remember, effective communication is not just about sending messages, it's about creating connections and building lasting relationships with your customers.

By taking the reins and becoming the conductor of your retail journey, you can ensure that your symphony continues to resonate, captivating customers and driving your business to new heights.

❑❑❑

CHAPTER 6

SHOWCASING

A Few Compelling Retail Case Studies

Here are a few case studies that illustrate the importance of various aspects of retail mastery in the Indian market, focusing on the Five Senses, Data Analytics, Staff Training & Power of Effective Communication in Retail.

Blackberrys - Crafting a Superior Retail Experience Through

- Sensory Engagement
- Staff Training
- Data Analytics &
- Communication

The Background

Blackberrys, established in 1991 by Mohan Clothing Co. Pvt Ltd., has grown into India's leading menswear brands. Known for its premium quality formal wear, casual wear, and accessories, Blackberrys caters to the modern Indian man with a focus on sophistication and style.

This case study explores how Blackberrys leverages the five senses, staff training, data analytics, and effective communication to create an exceptional retail experience.

Blackberrys did not opt for this approach as a solution to a challenge, rather it was their inherent vision and culture and they could be considered the pioneer of the service/experience-focused retail revolution.

Engaging the Five Senses in Blackberry Stores

1. **Sight**
    - **Elegant Store Design:** Blackberrys stores are designed with a sleek and modern aesthetic. Clean lines, well-lit interiors, and strategic product displays enhance the visual appeal and align with the brand's sophisticated image.
    - **Attention to Detail:** The visual merchandising is carefully curated, with a focus on highlighting the premium quality and craftsmanship of their garments. Seasonal collections are prominently displayed to attract customers' attention and showcase the latest trends.
2. **Sound**
    - **Ambient Music:** The stores play soft, contemporary music that complements the shopping experience. The choice of music is intended to create a calm and relaxed atmosphere, allowing customers to browse at their leisure.
    - **Brand-Consistent Soundscapes:** The background music aligns with Blackberrys brand identity, enhancing the overall ambience and making the shopping experience more enjoyable.
3. **Smell**
    - **Subtle Fragrances:** Blackberrys uses subtle and sophisticated fragrances in their stores to create a pleasant and inviting environment. The use of mild, fresh scents helps to reinforce the brand's focus on elegance and quality.
    - **Fragrance Consistency:** The consistent use of specific fragrances across stores helps create a familiar and cohesive brand experience for repeat customers.

4. **Touch**
    - **Product Interaction:** Customers are encouraged to touch and feel the fabrics of the garments. The tactile experience is crucial for appreciating the quality and comfort of Blackberrys clothing.
    - **Interactive Displays:** The stores feature interactive displays where customers can explore different textures and styles, making the shopping experience more engaging.
5. **Taste**
    - **Special Events and Promotions:** During special events, Blackberrys offers refreshments to customers, adding an element of hospitality to the shopping experience. While not a regular feature, these occasional treats contribute to a memorable retail experience.

Staff Training and Customer Interaction

Customer-Centric Training

Blackberrys places a strong emphasis on training their staff to provide exceptional customer service.

- **Product Knowledge:** Employees are trained extensively on the features, materials, and craftsmanship of Blackberrys products. This deep product knowledge enables them to offer informed recommendations and answer customer queries effectively.
- **Personalized Service:** Staff are trained to understand and cater to the individual needs of customers. This includes providing personalized styling advice and ensuring that each customer feels valued and attended to.

Interactive Engagement

Blackberrys encourages a high level of interaction between staff and customers.

- **Greeting and Assistance:** From the moment a customer enters the store, they are greeted and offered assistance. Staff are trained to be attentive without being intrusive, striking the right balance to enhance the shopping experience.
- **Building Relationships:** Regular customers are recognized and engaged in conversations about their preferences and past purchases, helping to build a strong customer relationship and loyalty.

Leveraging Data Analytics

Data-Driven Decisions

Blackberrys uses data analytics to optimize various aspects of their business, from inventory management to customer engagement.

- **Customer Insights:** By analyzing purchase history and customer preferences, Blackberrys tailors its product offerings and marketing efforts to meet the specific needs of its clientele.
- **Inventory Optimization:** Data analytics helps in forecasting demand and managing inventory levels efficiently, ensuring that popular items are always available and reducing the risk of overstock or stockouts.

Enhanced Marketing Strategies

Data insights are used to create targeted marketing campaigns.

- **Personalized Promotions:** Blackberrys uses data to identify customer segments and deliver personalized promotions and discounts, increasing the effectiveness of their marketing efforts.

- **Behavioral Analysis:** Understanding customer behavior patterns allows Blackberrys to optimize store layouts and product displays to better align with shopping habits and preferences.

Effective Communication Strategies

Multi-Channel Engagement

Blackberrys effectively uses various communication channels to connect with its customers and promote its brand.

- **Digital Presence:** The brand maintains a strong online presence through its website and social media platforms, where it shares updates on new collections, promotions, and fashion tips.
- **Loyalty Programs:** Blackberrys loyalty program rewards frequent shoppers with exclusive benefits, encouraging repeat purchases and fostering customer loyalty.

Brand Storytelling

Communication efforts at Blackberrys are focused on conveying the brand's values and story.

- **Content Marketing:** Through blogs, newsletters, and social media posts, Blackberrys shares content that highlights their commitment to quality, craftsmanship, and style. This storytelling approach helps to build a deeper connection with their audience.
- **Consistent Messaging:** Across all communication channels, Blackberrys maintains a consistent brand voice and message, reinforcing its identity and ensuring a cohesive customer experience.

The Spectacular Result

Blackberrys has successfully established itself as a leading menswear brand in India by creating a superior retail experience that engages the five senses, emphasizes exceptional customer service, leverages data analytics, and employs effective communication strategies.

Their approach to retail mastery not only enhances customer satisfaction but also drives loyalty and business growth.

This case study illustrates how Blackberrys excels in creating a memorable and engaging retail experience through a blend of sensory engagement, top-notch customer service, data-driven operations, and strategic communication.

Fabindia - The Raja of Its Niche

Company Background

Fabindia, founded in 1960, is a well-known Indian retail brand that specializes in traditional Indian clothing, accessories, and home furnishings. The brand is recognized for its focus on promoting Indian crafts and handlooms.

The Challenge

Fabindia faced the challenge of standing out in a competitive retail market dominated by both local and international players. They needed a strategy to attract customers and create a memorable shopping experience that would drive repeat visits and customer loyalty.

The Solution

Fabindia adopted a multi-sensory retail approach to create a rich and immersive shopping environment. Here's how they engaged the five senses:

Engaging the Five Senses

1. **Sight**
    - **Visual Merchandising:** Fabindia stores are designed to reflect traditional Indian aesthetics, using vibrant colors, handcrafted displays, and artistic décor that resonate with their brand's identity.
    - **Product Presentation:** The layout and presentation of products are carefully curated to highlight the craftsmanship and uniqueness of each item.
2. **Sound**
    - **Ambient Music:** Stores play soothing Indian classical or folk music that complements the brand's traditional theme and enhances the shopping experience.
3. **Smell**
    - **Scented Environment:** Fabindia uses natural scents like sandalwood or jasmine within their stores, creating a pleasant and inviting atmosphere that aligns with their focus on natural and organic products.
4. **Taste**
    - **Café Integration:** Some larger Fabindia stores include the Fab Café, offering organic and traditional Indian foods. This not only provides customers with a taste of India but also encourages them to spend more time in the store. Fabindia also offers customers complimentary samples of traditional Indian teas or snacks in some stores.
5. **Touch**
    - **Tactile Experience:** Customers are encouraged to touch and feel the fabrics and textures of products. The tactile engagement is crucial for a brand that sells handcrafted goods, as it allows customers to appreciate the quality and craftsmanship.

The Spectacular Results:

Fabindia's multi-sensory approach has been successful in creating a unique and engaging shopping experience. It has helped the brand maintain a strong market position and customer loyalty despite the influx of international competitors. The sensory-rich environment encourages customers to spend more time in stores, often leading to increased sales.

By effectively engaging all five senses, Fabindia has created a distinctive and memorable shopping experience that resonates deeply with its customers. This approach not only strengthens the brand's identity but also drives customer loyalty and repeat business.

❑❑❑

CHAPTER 7

THE RETAIL ALL-STARS

Assemble Your Winning Team!

Let's Begin, The END With a Story!

Once upon a time, there was a powerful king, he was not only powerful but extremely prosperous too. His life was adorned with all the trappings of success. Yet, he didn't feel happy and fulfilled, there was a continuous sense of restless yearning for something more flickered within him, and he wanted more out of his life.

So, he embarked on a grand exploration, a journey to discover joy and fulfillment. He had one of the finest chariots in the entire region, driven by powerful, rare-bred horses.

The king was sure with the mighty chariot and the amazing horses he would soon find his destination and the road to discovery would be a grand adventure.

However, to his shock and surprise instead of racing forward smoothly, his chariot merely crawled forward in a rough and bumpy manner.

His prized steeds were all eager to propel him towards the horizon. But despite their combined might, the chariot barely crawled forward.

> The king wondered why, so he went and stood at the helm of the chariot and carefully watched the horses, he was surprised to see that each of the horses was trying to pull the chariot in a different direction that they felt was the best path for their beloved king. The loyal horses, each fixated on their interpretation of the "best path," pulled in conflicting directions, sadly instead of getting results, their efforts canceling each other out despite their noble intentions.
>
> Frustrated, the king dismounted. He approached each magnificent creature, whispering a single, crucial instruction into their ears. A profound transformation unfolded within a few minutes
>
> The horses, once disparate in their desires, aligned themselves in perfect unison.
>
> Their harnessed strength propelled the chariot forward with exhilarating speed, leaving the king breathless and excited in anticipation of the journey ahead and the journey invigorated.

This, dear reader, is the tale of many retailers. Your store might boast exceptional products, passionate staff, and a captivating brand, yet growth remains stagnant. Like the king's chariot, **your efforts lack synergy.**

Each element, though valuable, operates in isolation, hindering your journey towards success.

You've embarked on a captivating journey, exploring the four wheels of retail excellence.

We've delved deep into the 4 Wheels of Retail Excellence, namely:

- Visual Merchandising (The Play of the 5 Senses)
- The Art of Story Telling and ways to build a great story along with the spark that ignites sales through staff training,
- The power of data-driven insights, and
- The harmonious symphony of effective communication.

This book has been your map and compass, guiding you through the four wheels aligned to retail success: captivating visuals, empowered staff, data-driven insights, and strategic communication.

However, the journey doesn't end here. The real test lies in **implementing these strategies** and witnessing their transformative impact on your business. With all the strategies and information I've shared, I am sure you'll do a good job of it.

There's a crucial choice before you.

The knowledge you've gained is your starting point. Now comes the most crucial step: **implementation.**

Do you yearn for incremental progress by going it alone, or do you crave exponential growth?

If the latter resonates with you, then I invite you to join me on the next leg of your retail journey.

I understand that every retail business is unique. That's why I take a **personalized approach,** working closely with you to understand your specific needs, challenges, and goals. I'll then tailor my services to create a **comprehensive strategy** that addresses your unique situation and helps you achieve your desired outcomes.

Here's what I will do for you

- **Identify your unique retail goals.** What does success look like for you?Assess your current state. How well are you leveraging each of the four wheels?
- **Develop a strategic plan.** Identify areas for improvement and create actionable steps.
- **Provide proven strategies:** I've helped numerous retailers achieve their goals, and I can do the same for you.

Remember, achieving lasting success in retail requires **continuous learning, adaptation, and a commitment to excellence. By taking charge and strategically aligning your retail wheels,** you can turn your vision into reality, leaving the competition in the dust and steering your business towards a thriving future.

Ready to embark on your journey? We're here to help. Contact us today to discuss your specific needs and explore how we can partner with you to achieve your retail goals.

Schedule a free consultation at amit@facetsgroup.net to discuss your unique goals and discover how my expertise can help you **transform your retail vision into reality.**

Wishing you phenomenal growth

Happy Selling!!!

❑❑❑